ON A FOOD STAMP BUDGET

GUIDE TO AFFORDABLE MIXED CUISINE

By
Aqueelah

PublishAmerica
Baltimore

ISBN: 1-4241-9114-9
PUBLISHED BY PUBLISHAMERICA, LLLP
www.publishamerica.com
Baltimore

Printed in the United States of America

ON A FOOD STAMP BUDGET

GUIDE TO AFFORDABLE MIXED CUISINE

By

Aqueelah

A REMEMBRANCE OF ENCOURAGEMENT

BE KIND TO YOUR HEART
DO RIGHT BY YOUR MIND
BE STRONG
NEVER FALL WEAK
AND MOST OF ALL
STAY POSITIVE

Keep your mind focused on your goals.
When you set your mind to do something, to become someone never change that mindset.
Always no matter what stay on the right path and when you find your mind drifting down the stream in the wrong direction just look inside your heart and follow it home.
Always consider compromise.
Never doubt yourself for if you do you will be doubting your lively hood, your worth and we all know that you are worth more than gold.
You should try never to put yourself in a situation that you cannot handle.
Always hold true to your faith and beliefs for they are the foundations on which you base your life.
Remember that God loves you and wants the best for you just never let go of your faith and worship of him.
Times may be hard now and they may get worse before they get better but everything will be okay
Just remember to
BE KIND TO YOUR HEART
DO RIGHT BY YOUR MIND
BE STRONG
NEVER FALL WEAK
AND MOST OF ALL
STAY POSITIVE
FOR GOD HAS BLESSED YOU TO COME THIS FAR AND IT IS ONLY THE BEGINNING WITH MUCH MORE TO COME

On a Food Stamp Budget A Guide to Affordable Fine Mixed Cuisine is an exciting new cook book that teaches people just because you may be on food stamps or have a very low budget when it comes to food does not mean that you can't eat good, healthy, delicious meals. Nontraditional southern foods are the focus recipes in this cookbook. Throughout the cookbook it has tips to make your culinary experience more enjoyable, such as: time saving tips, things you should keep in your pantry, and of course tips to help save you money. Recipes for BBQ Turkey Meatloaf, Seared Saffron Chicken w/ Sun dried tomatoes, Candied Yams, Zucchini & Tomatoes, Hungarian Potatoes, and Crawfish Etoufee (I'm hungry just thinking about it) are examples of the wide variety of foods that can be cooked *ON A Food Stamp Budget*. I have infused my background of being a mother of three, a wife on a budget, biology major, and a personal chef into this cookbook. Using tips and recipes that have helped my family, my clients, and myself over the years I am now able to spread the knowledge and the joy on to you (which is very exciting to me to say the least)! It is a refreshingly unique and original cookbook that is a joy to read. It has poetry, tips, and recipes. The cookbook is unique in that not only does it appeal to all classes (upper, middle, and lower) it also appeals to all diversity backgrounds offering delicious, planned meals, that are quick, healthy, time saving, and most of all done On A Food Stamp Budget.

Aqueelah

DINNER MENU FOR ONE MONTH

WEEK 1

1. Black eyed peas w/ smoked turkey necks over rice w/ corn bread & stewed pole beans
2. BBQ turkey meat loaf w/ buttered rice and succotash
3. Crawfish Etoufee over grits
4. Seasoned Basil Chicken w/ Mandarin orange and pecan salad
5. Chili over rice w/ corn bread
6. Penne Pasta w/ marinara sauce and garden salad
7. Honey Rosemary Chicken w/ Creamed Potatoes and Zucchini & Tomatoes

WEEK 2

1. Sun dried tomato Chicken w/ sour cream & cream cheese potatoes and cauliflower
2. Supreme Red Beans and rice w/ green beans and Corn bread
3. Philly Cheese Steaks w/ Home made fries
4. Turkey Lasagna Rolls and Steamed Broccoli
5. BBQ Wings w/ Roasted Potatoes and Coleslaw
6. Spinach & Mushroom Salmon w/ Wild Rice Pilaf
7. Navy Bean Soup w/ Rice

WEEK 3

1. BBQ Salmon and Tossed Feta cheese salad
2. Fried Chicken w/ Macaroni and Cheese, Candied Yams and California blend vegetables (carrots,broccoli,cauliflower)
3. Pepper & Onion Steak w/ Rosemary Potatoes and Roasted Broccoli
4. Chicken Fettuccini Alfredo w/ Steamed Broccoli
5. Lima Beans over rice w/ green beans
6. Honey lemon Tilapia w/ Blue Cheese Tossed Salad
7. Oven BBQ Chicken w/ potato salad and Beet salad

WEEK 4

1. Three pepper chicken w/ Hungarian Potatoes and Squash & Zucchini Medley
2. Black Beans and Yellow rice w/ fried corn bread
3. Spinach & Mushroom Quesadeas w/ black bean salsa
4. Honey lemon Chicken w/ cream spinach and Greek Potatoes
5. BBQ & Provolone Turkey Burgers w/ Baked Beans
6. Oven Roast w/ Cream Potatoes and Stewed Green Beans
7. Baked Spaghetti w/ Grilled Zucchini and Garlic bread

WEEK 1

BLACK EYED PEAS AND SMOKED TURKEY NECKS

1 bag of black eyed peas
1 whole onion small diced
1 whole bell pepper small diced
1 quart chicken broth
1/2 quart water
1 ½ tsp cayenne pepper
Salt to taste
1 lb smoked turkey necks

Pour entire bag of peas into a large pot
Add water and chicken broth
Bring to a boil
Reduce heat and let simmer
Add onions, bell peppers, and salt
Let cook for about and hour and a half
Add smoked turkey necks
Cover and let cook for about another hour or until tender
Serve over rice and enjoy

POLE BEANS (SNAP BEANS)

1 lb of Pole beans
½ onion sliced long ways
1 quart chicken or vegetable broth
½tbs kosher salt
¼tsp cayenne pepper
2tbs butter (always optional)
TIP: you can use a buttered flavored spray to take the place of butter
or margarine
Margarine also has less fat

In a saucepan add pole beans
Pour chicken broth or vegetable broth on top
Add sliced onions, salt, pepper, and butter
Cover and let simmer till tender yet firm
Normally takes about 15 mins on medium high heat.

Tip: Instead of using chicken broth or vegetable broth you can use a
bouillon cube and just drop it into the dish that you are cooking, or
add one cube per 8oz of water to dilute.
Over cooking your vegetables takes all the nutrition out of your
vegetables.

CORN BREAD

1 ½ cups cornmeal
1 cup all purpose flour
¼ cup sugar
1 cup of milk
¾ cups peanut oil
2 eggs

In a bowl add all ingredients
Mix well
Spray a cooking spray into bottom of cast iron skillet
Pour Mixture into skillet
Bake on 325 degrees for 25 mins
Serve and enjoy

BBQ TURKEY MEATLOAF

2 lbs of ground turkey
1 ½ cups salsa
2 eggs
1 ½ tbs salt
1 tsp cayenne pepper
1tsp garlic powder
2 tsp oatmeal

In a large bowl add ground turkey, salsa, salt, pepper, garlic powder,
eggs, and oatmeal.
Mix well with hands
Mold into a loaf
Transfer to loaf pan
Bake in oven on 350 degrees for 45-60 mins
Top with BBQ Sauce

TIP: Ground turkey is cheaper than ground beef and leaner.
It also tastes really good!

SUCCOTASH

Two ears of corn cleaned and kernels taken off
Twelve fresh okra sliced
One cup of onions medium diced
30 oz of whole peeled tomatoes (crushed in hands)

In a pan saute onions for 2 mins in olive oil
Mix in corn and okra
Cook for 2 mins
Pour tomatoes in pan
Blend well
Salt to taste
Cook for 8-10mins on low heat till tender.

CRAWFISH ETOUFEE

2 ½ lbs of crawfish
1-½ cups small-diced onions
1 ½ cup small-diced Anaheim peppers
1-½ cups small diced green bell peppers
32oz crushed tomatoes
16oz whole tomatoes (crush in hands)
½ cup Old Bay Seasoning
2tsp Cayenne pepper
2tbs Olive oil
1 ½ tsp kosher salt

In a stock pot sauté onions, bell peppers, and Anaheim peppers in olive oil for 2-3 mins
Add Crawfish tails, Old Bay Seasoning, Cayenne Pepper, and tomatoes
Salt to taste
Stir together and let cook on medium heat till it boils then reduce heat and let simmer for 15mins
Serve over grits

TIP: Most people serve Crawfish etoufee over rice but I am a southern girl and I love grits and Crawfish etoufee taste excellent over grits! Trust me!

SEASONED BASIL CHICKEN

4 Boneless skinless chicken breast
3tbs olive oil
½ tbs distilled vinegar
3 tbs honey
1tbs lemon pepper
½ tbs garlic powder
1tbs dried basil
Salt to taste

In a large bowl add olive oil, vinegar, honey, lemon pepper, garlic powder, dried basil, and salt
Blend olive oil mixture well
Dip chicken breast in olive oil mixture and coat well
Put chicken breast on a baking sheet and bake in oven on 325 degrees for 45mins to an hour or till tender.

TIP: When blending oils and herbs and spices together it is called a rub. Rubs are great because they help to coat the food evenly and help you preserve your spices longer!

MANDARAIN ORANGE & PECAN TOSSED SALAD

3 cups of baby spinach
2 cups of green leaf lettuce
1 ½ cups mandarin oranges
½ cup toasted pecans
¼ cup shredded Parmesan cheese
10 grape tomatoes

In a large bowl add in ingredients
Top with citrus vinaigrette

CHILI

1lb ground turkey
1 bag of Kidney beans
2 Anaheim peppers small diced
1 onion small diced
1 bell pepper small diced
1 small can of diced tomatoes
2tsp Cayenne Pepper
2oz Chili powder
2tbs minced garlic

In a stock pot cook Kidney beans according to package
Add chili powder, garlic powder, and cayenne pepper
Cook ground turkey mixture and add minced garlic, bell peppers,
Anaheim peppers, onions and tomatoes
Add ground turkey mixture to Kidney beans after about 45 minutes
of cooking beans
Let simmer till thickened
Serve with rice and corn bread and enjoy

PENNE PASTA
W/ MARINARA SAUCE

1lb Penne pasta
24oz Marinara sauce
Grated Parmesan cheese (as much as you like)

Cook pasta according to package
Cook marinara sauce according to recipe
Do not rinse pasta
Plate pasta and top with marinara sauce and grated parmesan cheese

TIP: When it comes to cheese you can never have enough!

GARDEN SALAD

3 Cups Romine lettuce shredded
3 Hard boiled eggs chopped
½ cup Mild Shredded Cheddar Cheese
½ cup Pineapple Tidbits
1 cup Croutons
1 cup Cucumbers sliced thin

In a large bowl combine above ingredients
Top with your favorite Salad dressing

HONEY ROSEMARY CHICKEN

1 whole chicken cut up into 8 pieces
4tbs Olive Oil
3tbs dried rosemary
½ tsp Cayenne pepper
3tbs honey
1 ½ tbs salt
½ tbs distilled vinegar

In a bowl make a wet rub with Olive oil, vinegar, honey, garlic
powder, cayenne pepper, and salt
Blend well
Dip chicken in rub and coat chicken well
Sprinkle Rosemary over chicken
Put chicken in a roasting pan and cook on 325 degrees for 45 mins

CREAM POTATOES

2.5lbs Red Potatoes
1/3 pint of heavy cream
½ stick of butter or margarine
Salt to taste

In a pot cook potatoes till tender, then drain
In the same pot add heavy cream, butter and salt
Using a knife cut potatoes still leaving a little lumpy
Using a spoon blend together well

ZUCCHINI & TOMATOES

6 large Zucchini
2 Vidalia onions sliced long ways
1 cup diced tomatoes
1 ½ tsp salt
3 tbs Olive oil
¼ tsp cayenne pepper
In a large hot pan add Olive Oil
After oil becomes hot add onions and zucchini
Toss Zucchini and onions around for 4 mins
Add tomatoes, salt, and pepper
Serve and enjoy

WEEK 2

SUN DRIED TOMATO CHICKEN

1 chicken cut up into 8 pieces
1 bottle Sun dried tomato Vinaigrette
1 onion julienne
½ tsp cayenne pepper
2 tsp kosher salt
1tsp garlic powder

In a large bowl add chicken and vinaigrette
Let marinade for at least 4 hrs in the refrigerator
Put chicken in a roasting pan and add salt, pepper, garlic powder,
and onions
Let roast (cook uncovered) in oven for 45mins to an hour on 325
degrees or till tender

SOUR CREAM &
CREAM CHEESE POTATOES

2.5lbs of Yellow Golden Yukon Potatoes
4oz heavy cream
8oz cream cheese
8oz sour cream
2tbs butter or margarine
2tbs salt
1tsp white pepper

In a stock pot boil potatoes till tender
Drain potatoes
Put potatoes back into pot
Add heavy cream, sour cream, cream cheese, butter, salt and pepper
With a knife chop potatoes, then use spoon to stir till blended well

STEAMED CAULIFLOWER

1 head of Cauliflower
2 tsp salt
2 tbs butter or margarine
¼ tsp white pepper
2-4oz of water

Destem Cauliflower and cut off pieces
In a pot add water, salt, pepper and butter
Let water boil
Add Cauliflower and let cook uncovered for about 15 mins till
tender but not soggy

SUPREME RED BEANS AND RICE

12oz Red Kidney beans
2/3 cups small diced onions
3 cups Chicken broth or 3 bouillon cubes
Water
1tbs Cayenne pepper (I like them spicy)
½ lb smoked turkey necks
1 jalapeno pepper sliced
Salt to taste

In a stock pot mix in beans, broth, water, onions, salt, cayenne
pepper, jalapeno pepper, and turkey necks
Bring to a boil
Reduce heat cover and let simmer for about 4-5 hours
Serve over Uncle Bens Rice
Enjoy

TIP: I always put the water level about 2 inches above the beans to
allow them to cook for a longer time. I am always busy so I just set
them and go. Adding butter or margarine to this dish will add fabu-
lously extra flavor!! Trust me!

STEWED GREEN BEANS

1lb of green beans w/ ends taken off
½ onion julienne (sliced long ways)
1 medium size tomato diced (optional)
¼ tsp cayenne pepper
½ tsp garlic powder
1 quart chicken broth or vegetable broth

In a large skillet combine green beans, onions, tomato, salt, pepper,
garlic powder, and chicken broth
Cook on high till broth starts boil, then reduce heat to low and let
simmer covered for about 30 mins
Serve and enjoy

PHILLY CHEESESTEAKS

2lbs of Rib eye steak shaved thin
1 ½ onion sliced long ways
1 bell pepper sliced long ways
½ tsp cayenne pepper
1tsp garlic powder
2tbs Seasoned salt
¾ lbs of Baby Swiss cheese shredded
Six Hogi Buns

Slice buns in half and spray with butter flavored no stick cooking spray
Toast buns in oven
In a skillet cook steak with onion, bell peppers, garlic powder,
seasoned salt, and cayenne pepper
After buns are toasted put steak mixture in buns top with cheese
Serve and Enjoy

HOMEMADE FRIES

1 ½ lbs of potatoes
¼ cups of olive oil
1/8 cups of peanut oil
½ Vidalia onion Julienne
1tsp garlic powder
Salt to taste

Clean and cut potatoes
Cut into wedges
In a cast iron skillet pour in olive oil and peanut oil
Heat oil
Add onions and let cook for about 1 ½ minutes then add potatoes,
garlic powder, and salt
Pan fry till potatoes are brown and crispy on both sides

TIP: When making home made fries I like to use a regular Russet
potato over any other kind because they fry better.

TURKEY LASAGNA ROLLS

1 box of Lasagna noodles
1lb of ground turkey
½ green bell pepper small diced
½ fresh onion minced
About 2 cups of Marinara sauce
1 cup of Mozzarella and Parmesan Cheese blend
½ cup Ricotta cheese
About 2 tsp salt
1 tsp Garlic powder

In a pot of boiling water cook Lasagna noodles according to package
In a skillet cook ground turkey, bell pepper, onion, salt, garlic powder till meat is no longer pink
Drain turkey and put in a bowl; add Ricotta cheese to mixture
After noodles are done roll turkey and Ricotta mixture in each noodle individually
Top with marinara sauce and cheese blend
Put in oven on 350 degrees or 7 mins or until cheese melts

STEAMED BROCCOLI

2 heads of Broccoli
1tbs butter
Salt to taste

In a pot put about 3tbs water in the pot
Turn pot on high and add salt
Cut broccoli steams off only leaving the florets (the tops)
Let water start to boil then add Florets and butter
Cover and let cook on high for about 5 mins

TIP: Remember we want the vegetable firm and tender. Not soggy!

BBQ WINGS

1 Package chicken wings
½ green bell pepper sliced
½ onion sliced
1tbs Seasoning Salt
½ tsp garlic powder
1 bottle BBQ Sauce

Clean chicken
In a Roasting pan add wings
Season chicken with Seasoning salt and garlic powder
Add bell peppers and onions
Put chicken in oven on 350 degrees for 35 mins
After 35 mins take chicken out and add BBQ sauce
Continue to let cook and additional 25 mins

TIP: When cooking any type of poultry I try to keep a thermometer around so that I can check the temp on my poultry. You want the temp to be at least 180-185 degrees to make sure that it is done.

ROASTED POTATOES W/ CHEESE

2.5lbs of potatoes sliced thin
4tbs Olive oil
2tbs salt
½ tsp black pepper (Surprised!)
1 cup of onions julienne
½ cup mild shredded cheddar cheese

In a bowl coat potatoes with olive oil, salt, and pepper
Transfer potatoes to a roasting pan and top with onions
Bake on 325 degrees for about an hour and a half
Top with cheese

TIP: I normally do not use black pepper mainly because you cannot digest it. In this dish I do simply because I like the taste of it over any other pepper I use. A roasting pan is just simply a pan deeper than a baking sheet.

COLE SLAW

4 cups shredded cabbage
1 cup shredded carrots
¼ cup shallots
¾ cups mayo
3 tbs vinegar
1 ½ tbs sugar
1 ½ tbs mustard
2 tsp salt

In a bowl mix mayo, sugar, garlic powder, and salt together
In another bowl put in cabbage and carrots
Pour mayo mixture over cabbage mixture; stir together.
Add vinegar over Cole slaw
Blend well
Serve and enjoy

SPINACH AND MUSHROOM SALMON

6 4oz pieces of Salmon
1 can of spinach drained
10 button mushrooms sliced
6oz diced tomatoes
1 bottle Sun dried tomato vinaigrette
½ bottle balsamic vinaigrette
2 oz honey

In a bowl mix drained spinach with mushrooms and tomatoes
Mix in 1tbs Sun dried tomato vinaigrette into spinach mixture
Marinade Salmon filets in Sun dried tomato and balsamic vinaigrette
for at least 4 hours
After marinating Salmon top with spinach mixture
Individually wrap Salmon in foil
Drizzle Salmon with honey
On a baking sheet broil Salmon on 350 degrees for 5-7 mins
Serve over rice

WILD RICE PILAF

2 Cups Wild Rice
2tbs butter
¼ cup fresh minced onions
½ cup diced button mushrooms
1 quart chicken broth

In a hot pan add butter and onions together
Let sauté for about 30 seconds then add rice and mushrooms
Let sauté for about an additional 30 seconds together then add chicken broth
Transfer rice to a roasting pan and let cook in oven for about 20 minutes on 300 degrees or till tender

TIP: Or just let the rice cook in the pan w/ lid on, on a low heat till done.

NAVY BEAN SOUP

8oz of Navy Beans
2/3 cups small diced onions
½ cup sliced celery
½ cup sliced carrots
1 ½ tbs kosher salt
Water
½ quart vegetable stock or 2 bouillon cubes

In a large pot pour in beans and add in onions, celery, carrots,
stock and salt
Add enough water to just cover the beans
Cook on high till beans start to boil then reduce heat and let simmer
for about an hour and a half
Let beans cook till there is a little liquid left
If you have a bean strainer then strain your beans; if not then take a
fork and mash beans till there are no more lumps and beans are well
blended or put beans in a blender
Serve over rice and enjoy

WEEK 3

BBQ SALMON

4 4oz Salmon filets
4oz of BBQ Sauce
2 tbs kosher salt
½ tsp cayenne pepper
1 ½ tsp garlic powder
½ tbs lemon pepper

Season Salmon with salt, pepper, garlic powder, and lemon pepper
In a roasting pan lay seasoned Salmon w/ BBQ sauce in pan (coat
pan with non stick cooking spray)
Broil on 350 degrees for 5-7 mins
Serve and Enjoy

TOSSED SALAD W/ FETA CHEESE

3 cups Romaine lettuce
1 cup of Red Leaf lettuce
½ cup Feta cheese crumbles
A handful of Cherry tomatoes
¼ cup Almonds

In a bowl add lettuce, feta crumbles, tomatoes, and almonds
Toss together
Serve w/ Dressing of choice

FRIED CHICKEN

1 cut up chicken
1 ½ tbs Seasoning salt
1 tsp garlic powder
½ tsp cayenne pepper
1 cup flour
1 plastic grocery bag
About 3 cups Peanut Oil

In a hot cast iron skillet pour Peanut oil
Let oil Get hot (make sure your fire is on a medium high flame)
In the plastic bag add cleaned chicken and season chicken with salt,
garlic powder and cayenne pepper
Add flour to chicken close bag and toss chicken around till well
coated with flour
Add chicken to hot grease and cut flame down to medium heat
Add bigger pieces first because they tend to take longer to cook
Let chicken cook for about 8 minutes on each side then turn over
and repeat
After chicken is finish cooking place on a brown paper bag or
napkin to let drain

TIP: When frying chicken you can listen to the chicken to tell when
it is done. When the chicken starts to have a simmering sound then it
is done. Or when the chicken starts to float a little it is done.

MACARONI AND CHEESE

12oz medium size shells
6oz heavy cream
1tbs minced fresh onions
3tbs butter (optional)
6oz mild cheddar cheese
6oz mozzarella cheese
2oz bread crumbs (sauté in butter)
Salt to taste

Cook shells according to package
Drain shells (do not rinse)
In the same pot that you cooked shells in add cooked shells back to
pot and add in cream, butter, onions, cheese and salt
Mix together
In a roasting pan add cheese to bottom of pan then add shells top
with cheese and sauté bread crumbs
Bake on 350 degrees for 15 mins or until cheese melts

CANDIED YAMS

2 medium size cans of yams
½ box dark brown sugar
½ cup of honey
3tbs of butter

Combine yams, brown sugar, honey, and butter together in a pan
Let yams boil then reduce heat and let simmer for about 15 mins

TIP: Feel free to use fresh yams and sweet potatoes. To make it easy on
your self boil the fresh yams and sweet potatoes first then peel them.

CALIORNIA BLEND VEGETABLES

1 bag of frozen California blend vegetables
2tbs butter
1tsp salt

In a pot add enough water to just cover the bottom of pot
Add salt to water and butter
Let water start to boil
add about 3 cups of vegetables
Cover and let cook on medium heat for about 15 minutes

PEPPER AND ONION STEAK

1 whole onion small diced
1 whole green bell pepper small diced
2 ½ inch Rib Eye Steaks
½ tsp garlic powder
1 ½ tbs seasoned salt
¼ tsp cayenne pepper
2 tsp olive oil

Coat steaks with oil
Season steaks with salt, pepper, garlic powder
In a Ziploc bag put your steaks in and add onions and bell peppers

ROSEMARY POTATOES

2.5lbs new baby potatoes cut in halve
3 stems of fresh Rosemary
4oz of Extra Virgin Olive Oil
Kosher salt to taste
¼ tsp cayenne pepper
2tbs butter or margarine

Boil potatoes till tender but not falling apart
Drain potatoes
In a large pot coat potatoes with olive oil, rosemary, butter, salt, and pepper
Blend well
Transfer to a serving dish and enjoy

TIP: If you have noticed I do not peel any of my potatoes because a lot of the nutrition in the potato comes from the skin.

ROASTED BROCCOLI

1lb Broccoli spears
3tbs Olive Oil
1tbs salt
¼ tsp Cayenne pepper
1 tsp chili powder
¼ tsp Grill seasoning

In a pot of roaring boiling water cook broccoli for 3 mins
Take broccoli out and transfer to a large bowl
In another bowl add olive oil, salt, cayenne pepper, chili powder,
garlic powder, grill seasoning and with a whip blend well
Place broccoli on a baking sheet and pour Olive oil mixture on top
Mix together with hands making sure broccoli is well coated
Broil in oven for 10mins on 325 degrees or till tender

CHICKEN FETTUCCINI ALFREDO

4 Boneless Skinless Chicken Breast Salted and Medium Diced
1lb Fettuccini
1 ½ cup Alfredo Sauce

Boil Fettuccini according to package
Drain Fettuccini (do not rinse)
Plate dish as follows: Fettuccini, Chicken, Alfredo Sauce

LIMA BEANS

1 bag of Lima Beans
1/3 cup diced green bell pepper
½ cup onions small diced
½ cup celery small diced
Salt to taste
2 tsp White pepper
½ quart chicken stock
1 quart water

In a large pot pour entire bag of beans in pot
Add chicken stock and enough water top cover beans (about 2 inches above beans)
Add celery, salt, pepper, onions, and bell pepper
Cook on high till beans start to boil then reduce heat and let simmer for about an hour and a half

TIP: When ever you bake or boil your chicken save the juice from it and strain it. The juice from your own chicken makes a delicious stock and taste better than what they sell in the stores. You can store it in the freezer until you get ready to use it again. Oh! It makes your cornbread dressing taste wonderful.

HONEY LEMON TILAPIA

6 pieces of Tilapia filets
3tbs lemon pepper
2tbs honey
2oz Olive oil
1tsp garlic powder
½ lemon

In a bowl make a wet rub using Olive Oil,
salt, lemon pepper, honey, and garlic powder
Blend well in a bowl
Dip Tilapia in rub then place Tilapia in a pan and bake on 325
degrees for about 5 mins
After 5 mins squeeze lemon juice on fish
and place back in oven for 5 mins

BLUE CHEESE TOSSED SALAD

4 cups Green Leaf lettuce shredded
A handful of Grape tomatoes
¾ Cup Blue Cheese Crumbles
1 cup Garlic Style Croutons
Russian dressing

In a bowl mix together lettuce, tomatoes, blue cheese, and croutons
Top with Russian dressing

OVEN BBQ CHICKEN

1 chicken cut up into 8 pieces
2 tbs salt
1 ½ tsp cayenne pepper
2 cups Char Grill BBQ Sauce
3 tbs honey
1tsp garlic powder

Clean chicken
In a bowl season chicken with salt, cayenne pepper, garlic powder,
and honey
Transfer chicken from bowl to a roasting pan
Roast chicken for about 30 mins on 325 degrees
After 30 mins take chicken out and add BBQ sauce
Cook for an additional 20-30 mins
Serve and enjoy

Marinade for at least 4 hrs in refrigerator
Broil steaks for 5-7 mins on each side on 325 degrees
You should wrap each steak individually in aluminum foil

POTATO SALAD

2lbs of potatoes
2 cups of mayo
3tbs of mustard
2tbs of sweet relish
6 hard boiled eggs shelled
1tbs salt
¼ tsp cayenne pepper

In two separate pots boil potatoes till tender and boil eggs for about
8-10 mins
After potatoes and eggs are done drain potatoes and eggs
In a large bowl add potatoes and eggs
With a knife chop potatoes and eggs
Add unopened room temp mayo to potatoes and eggs
Add mustard, sweet relish, salt and pepper
With a large spoon mix well
Refrigerate and serve cold

BEET SALAD

2 cans of cut up beets drained
½ cup of mayo
1 tbs distilled vinegar
1 tsp salt
½ tsp white pepper
2 hard boiled eggs shelled and diced

In a bowl add beets, mayo, eggs, vinegar, salt and pepper
With a large spoon blend well
Refrigerate and enjoy

WEEK 4

THREE PEPPER CHICKEN

4 Boneless Skinless Chicken Breast
1 yellow bell pepper julienne
1 orange bell pepper julienne
1 red bell pepper julienne
3tbs honey
Salt to taste
½ tsp Cayenne Pepper

Using Saran wrap and a mallet take chicken one at a time and wrap
in Saran wrap and pound out chicken with a mallet till you can get it
as thin as possible
Take chicken out of Saran wrap and place in a pan
Take bell peppers and put about 1 of each color pepper on the edge
of chicken then pour honey and season with salt and pepper
Roll chicken up making sure peppers stay inside
Dip chicken in Olive Oil
Place chicken on cookie sheet and cook for about 40 mins till done

HUNGARIAN POTATOES

2 ½ lbs of white potatoes sliced into wedges
14pz of canned whole tomatoes (crush in hands)
1 whole onion sliced long ways
2tbs butter
12oz Vegetable or chicken broth

In a pot combine potatoes, tomatoes, onions, butter and vegetable
broth and cover
Cook on medium heat till potatoes are tender and sauce thickened
Serve and enjoy

SQUASH & ZUCCHINI MEDLEY

3 large squash
3 large zucchini
1 Vidalia onions julienne
6 slices turkey bacon cut into thin slices
2 tbs Olive oil

Slice squash and zucchini in halve long ways and then cut halves
into one inch thick pieces
Put squash and zucchini in pot of boiling water for 2-3 mins
In a hot pan add Olive oil and let oil get hot then add bacon and onions
With a slotted spoon take vegetables out of water and place in pan
with onions and bacon
Toss vegetables around in pan for 3 mins or till tender yet firm
Salt to taste

TIP: A slotted spoon is just a large spoon with holes in them. Squash
also taste really good with a red bell pepper and turkey bacon added
to it!

BLACK BEANS

2 14oz cans of black beans
½ cup small diced onions
½ tsp minced garlic
½ tsp cayenne pepper
1 tbs Olive Oil
1 tbs Salt

In a pot sauté onions and garlic
Pour in black beans and add salt and cayenne pepper
Cook on medium heat for 15 mins
Serve over yellow or white rice

YELLOW RICE

1 bag Yellow rice
2tbs Olive oil

Follow directions on the back of the bag

TIP: Zatarains make really good yellow rice mixture.

FRIED CORNBREAD (Corn Cakes)

Use cornbread recipe
Peanut Oil

In a cast iron skillet add about one tbs oil
Let oil get hot and add corn bread mixture (cook like you cook
pancakes)
Have flame on medium heat
Let cornbread mixture harden on one side then flip
Turn over and let cook on other side
Drain on paper towels
Serve and enjoy

SPINACH AND MUSHROOM QUESADILLAS

4 large Tortilla shells
1 8oz package of button mushrooms sliced
1 package of baby spinach
2 cups shredded pepper jack cheese
½ onion sliced long ways
2 tbs olive oil
¼ tsp white pepper
Salt to taste

In a pan heat oil and mix together mushrooms, onions, spinach, salt, and pepper
Heat griddle over medium heat and add a little olive oil to griddle
Add tortilla
Cook tortilla one minute then turn it over
Sprinkle ¼ cup cheese and ¼ cup spinach mixture over ½ of the tortilla then fold the plain half of the tortilla over he top of the filling and gently press down with a spatula
Cook the quesadeas about 30 secs or till lightly browned and cheese melts
Remove quesadeas to a cutting service and cut into wedges
Serve and enjoy

BLACK BEAN SALSA

1-14oz can of black beans
1 8oz can of sweet corn drained
4oz diced tomatoes
2 Anaheim peppers deseeded and sliced
1 jalapeno pepper sliced
1 minced garlic clove
About 2tbs Olive oil

Sauté Anaheim peppers, onions, garlic, and jalapeno peppers together
Pour in black beans, corn and tomatoes
Blend together well
Cook on medium heat till heated through out

HONEY LEMON CHICKEN

6 Boneless Skinless Chicken Breast
3tbs Olive Oil
½ tbs distilled vinegar
5tbs honey
2tbs lemon juice
1tbs salt
½ tbs garlic powder
¼ cayenne pepper

In a bowl mix in olive oil, vinegar, honey, lemon juice, salt, garlic powder, cayenne pepper till blended
Dip chicken in wet rub till well coated and place on baking sheet
Roast chicken in oven for 45 mins on 325 degrees till done

CREAM SPINACH

2 bags Baby Spinach
1tsp fresh minced garlic
1tbs butter
½ pint Heavy Whipping Cream
1oz Grated Parmesan Cheese
1tsp White Pepper
Pinch of salt
In a large sauce pan cook Spinach in about 2oz of water until tender
Drain water
Add Heavy cream, onions, butter, Parmesan cheese, pepper, and salt
Mix well
Cook on medium heat till sauce thickens

GREEK POTATOES

2 ½ lbs of Golden Yukon potatoes cut into 4's
1 ½ tbs Greek Seasoning
½ cup Sour cream
1/3 cup grated Parmesan cheese
Salt to taste

Boil potatoes till tender, drain
Mix in Greek Seasoning, Sour cream, Parmesan cheese and salt
Blend well
Eat and enjoy

TURKEY AND PROVOLONE BURGERS

2lbs ground turkey
1 cup small diced onions sauté
1 cup small diced bell pepper sauté
2tbs kosher salt
1tsp garlic powder
½ tsp cayenne pepper
½ lb provolone cheese
2tbs olive oil
2 eggs
BBQ sauce (as much as you like)

In a pan sauté onions and bell peppers together in olive oil for 203 mins or until tender
In a large bowl mix ground turkey, onions, bell peppers, salt, garlic powder, and cayenne pepper, and eggs
Shape turkey mixture into patties
In the same pan that you sauté the vegetables in add a little more oil (just enough to coat the pan); let oil heat up and add turkey patties
Pan fry patties till done
Top burgers with provolone and BBQ sauce
Bun Turkey burgers and enjoy

BAKED BEANS

2-28oz cans of Bush's Vegetarian Baked Beans
½ lb light brown sugar
1 cup honey
1lb ground turkey
¼ cup small diced onion
¼ cup small diced green bell pepper
¼ tsp garlic powder
¼ tsp cayenne pepper
¼ cup brown sugar
¼ cup BBQ sauce

In a pot cook ground turkey and add bell peppers, onions, cayenne
pepper, and garlic powder
Cook till ground turkey is no longer pink
Do not drain turkey. Add beans, honey, brown sugar, and BBQ
sauce
Blend Well
Cook on medium heat for 30 mins

OVEN ROAST

1 Bone in Roast
½ green bell pepper small diced
½ onion small diced
2 tbs salt
1 garlic clove minced
½ tsp cayenne pepper
½ tbs distilled vinegar
In a Roasting pan season Roast with salt and cayenne pepper
Using a knife dig little holes into the roast and stuff them with
onions, garlic, and green bell peppers
Put roast in roasting bag or cover with aluminum foil;
add vinegar to roast
Cook on 250 degrees for 6 hours or till tender

TIP: When it comes to cooking a Roast with the bone in it the longer
the bone the more tender the roast.

BAKED SPAGHETTI

1 box of Spaghetti
40oz of Marinara sauce
1 ½ cups of sliced mushrooms
1 cup of green bell peppers small diced
1 cup of onions minced
1lb of ground turkey 1tbs cayenne pepper
1 tsp salt
2tsp garlic powder
2tbs Italian seasoning
1 ½ lbs of Shredded Mozzarella, Mild Cheddar, and Parmesan cheese

Cook spaghetti noodles according to package and drain (do not rinse)
In a large skillet cook ground turkey mixture with green bell peppers,
onion, cayenne pepper, garlic powder, Italian seasoning, and salt
After ground turkey mixture is done and no longer pink add
Marinara sauce to mixture
In the same pot that the noodles are in add ground turkey mixture
Blend well with noodles
In a roasting pan take a handful of cheese and add to the bottom of pan
Layer spaghetti mixture with cheese ending with cheese
Bake in oven uncovered for about 25 mins or until cheese is melted
Serve and enjoy

GRILLED ZUCCHINI

4 large zucchini
Extra virgin olive oil
Salt to taste

Using a knife slice zucchini long ways discarding the ends
Season the Zucchini with salt and coat with Olive oil
Using a hot in door grill place zucchini on grill for about one minute
on each side or till tender and you see the grill marks
Plate and enjoy

EXTRAS

STRAWBERRY SALAD

4cups spinach leaves
1 cup sliced button mushrooms
1 ½ cups sliced strawberries
½ cup walnuts

In a bowl toss together spinach, mushrooms, strawberries, and walnuts

TIP: This salad goes good with a citrus vinaigrette.

CITRUS VINAIGRETTE

2tbs lemon juice
3/4cups orange juice
½ tsp garlic powder
1tsp minced onion
½ tsp cayenne pepper
4tbs olive oil
1 ½ tbs finely chopped basil

In a bowl combine lemon juice, orange juice, garlic, onions, salt, pepper, and olive oil
Blend well with wire whip
Add basil
Top with salad of your choice

ALFREDO SAUCE

1 pint heavy whipping cream
1tsp fresh minced onion
1tsp minced garlic
Pinch of salt
¼ cup grated Parmesan cheese
1tbs butter or margarine

In a pan add heavy whipping cream, onions, garlic, salt, parmesan
cheese and butter
Bring to a boil
Let simmer on low heat until sauce has thickened

LEMONADE

6 large lemons
1 ½ cups sugar
1 gallon warm water
1 gallon pitcher

In a gallon pitcher squeeze lemons into pitcher, add sugar and water
Stir until sugar dissolves and well blended
Refrigerate and serve cold

MARINARA SAUCE

2-14oz cans of crushed tomatoes
2cups small diced onions
1 cup small diced bell peppers
1 ½ minced garlic clove
4tbs Italian seasoning
2tsp cayenne pepper
2oz of sugar
Kosher salt to taste
2tbs Extra virgin olive oil
In a stock pot sauté onions, bell peppers, and garlic in olive oil
Stir in tomatoes, Italian seasoning, cayenne pepper, sugar, and salt
Bring to a boil
Cover and simmer for an ½ hour

SUN DRIED TOMATO TURKEY W/ BABY SWISS SANDWICH

1lb Sun dried tomato turkey deli sliced
½ lb Baby Swiss deli sliced
Tomato slices
Romaine lettuce
½ onion julienne
8 button mushrooms
2tbs Olive oil
Ranch dressing
Sara Lee Honey White Bread

In a pan sauté onions and mushrooms
Put 2oz of turkey on bread with cheese, onions, mushrooms, lettuce, tomatoes, and ranch dressing
Eat and enjoy

TIP: Taste even better with toasted bread and melted cheese. When going to the Deli if you like your cheese and meat cut thin then ask them to cut it on #1.

THREE PEPPER LAMB CHOPS

6 Lamb Chops
1 garlic clove minced
2tsp salt
¼ tsp cayenne pepper
1 sliced red, yellow, and green bell pepper
Extra virgin olive oil

In a hot pan coat bottom of pan with oil
Season chops with garlic, salt, cayenne pepper, and bell peppers
Cook on medium heat for six mins on each side or till done
Enjoy

SEARED CHICKEN W/ SAFFRON AND SUN DRIED TOMATOES

4 pieces Boneless Skinless Chicken Breast
2tbs Saffron
1tbs kosher salt
1tsp Cayenne pepper
2tsp garlic powder
5oz chicken broth
14oz whole tomatoes (crushed in hands)
6 Sun dried tomatoes
2tbs Olive Oil
1/2tbs Distilled Vinegar

Coat hot pot with Olive oil
Season chicken with salt cayenne pepper and garlic powder
After oil is heated add saffron to oil
Sauté for about 30 secs then place seasoned chicken, broth, tomatoes, and vinegar in pot
Let simmer for about 45 mins uncovered on medium heat
Serve and enjoy

CREAM CHEESE POUND CAKE

2 sticks of butter
3 cups of sugar
6 eggs
3 cups of flour
1tsp pure vanilla extract
16oz of cream cheese (2 packages)
½ tsp baking powder

Cream butter and sugar together (make sure to have butter at room temp)
Add eggs one at a time till blended well
Sift flour and baking powder together
Add flour and cream cheese alternately (starting with flour and ending with flour)
Add vanilla extract last and blend well
Bake at 320 degrees for 65-75 min (depending on how brown you would like it)

SWEET POTATO PIE

4 Sweet Potatoes
3 Pie Shells
2 cups brown sugar
¾ cups sugar
2 sticks of butter (room temp)
1 cup Margarine
4tsp Cinnamon
2tsp Nutmeg
2 ½ tsp lemon extract
2 ½ tsp Vanilla Extract

Pre-heat oven to 350 degrees and
place pie shells in the oven for 5 minutes
Cook sweet potatoes till tender then peel
In a blender add sugar and butter and margarine
Blend together
Add Sweet Potatoes, lemon extract, cinnamon, nutmeg, and vanilla
Blend well for five minutes
Add filling to pie shells
Bake in oven for 20 minutes
Let cool and enjoy

TIPS

In this cook book through different recipes I have little tips that I put in to help your cooking experience more enjoyable. Now I want to give you little tips on things that you should keep in your pantry and refrigerator. First let me tell you to make something taste really good you do not have to be really extravagant with the ingredients; make it simple and easy. Okay now you should always try to keep potatoes around. Potatoes come in handy with a lot of different menus. I also like to keep canned tomatoes, fresh tomatoes, all kinds of fresh vegetables, and fruits. To be more specific: fresh green beans, broccoli, cauliflower, carrots, baby carrot (are great for snacking on) cucumbers, celery, bell peppers, okra, squash and onions. Keeping these items around will save you money and time in the grocery store. I also love fresh fruit. I love to keep bananas around, lemons, apples, oranges, grapefruit, and grapes! Do not forget rice. I love Uncle Bens Rice and Basmati rice! You should also keep varies types of dried beans and peas around, they always come in handy when your funds are looking low and when cooked right are very delicious.

Honey is a must. As well as olive oil, vinegar, and peanut oil. Honey taste really good on meats and olive oil and peanut oil are good for my wet rubs. I use a lot of vinegar in my meats to because vinegar is an acid and it helps to make my meats more tender. You can get all kinds of vinegars in the store. Balsamic and Red Wine Vinegar are other types of vinegar that you should try out some times.

Try to keep spices and herbs around too. Salt, pepper, garlic powder, minced garlic, Italian seasoning, Italian dressing, Vinaigrettes, Thyme, Sage, Seasoning salt, Lemon pepper, Chili powder, Basil, Rosemary,

Parsley just to name a few. If you are (or if your not) familiar with a lot of herbs do what I do and try to but a new spice or herb every week and try it in a new or old dish to see how you like it. Bouillon Cubes are a must to keep around. They add extra flavor to anything and comes in handy when you need a quick broth.

I chose to write this cookbook because I felt like people needed to know that just because you have a tight spending budget when it comes to food that you can still eat good, eat healthy, and all do it in a timely manner. I felt like up until now no one has done this. What makes my cookbook different from others is that I appeal to all classes: poor, middle class, and rich. No matter what your budget is, no matter your back ground the recipes in this cook book appeal to everyone. Being a mother of three, a wife, a personal chef, and a student my life could get pretty hectic at times. I have combined my skills of being a personal chef and a mom on a budget into one cookbook. These tips have helped myself, my clients, and my family out a tremendous amount. I feel like when you find something that is good and it works then spread the joy, spread the knowledge, and I have done so in this cook book. I hope you enjoy these recipes as much as I have.

CPSIA information can be obtained at www.ICGtesting.com
Printed in the USA
LVOW041035091211

258616LV00001B/108/P